the lovers

where she grows

to all the lovers I've ever loved

every lover held a mirror with all my
insecurities and loving them led to loving me.

I'd tell you that this is a work of fiction, but that
would be a lie. This book is a tale of lovers; the
loved, unloved, and unloving. I have been all three.
Based on true events. Some details and timelines
have been changed. Hope you hate it.

in the garden

******

the lovers

loving her

summer   pg. 7   bones   pg. 107

sunflowers   pg. 59   marigolds   pg. 167

the lovers

summer

I can feel the summer coming
he's in the rain and the morning light
while the meadowlarks sing the sun to the sky
he's in the fireflies that come out at night
while the cicada moan their lullabies
I can feel the summer coming
I've got my eyes on the sky and
I'm thirsty for the lightning to strike

I was trying to say goodbye
when you came rolling in
like a summer storm over the prairie
all thunder and heat
blowing down the covers and
climbing in my sheets
picking wildflowers from my body and
leaving kisses on my thighs
I was trying to say goodbye
when you came rolling in
like a summer storm over the prairie

I'm breathing air for the first time
shallow inhales
afraid that if I breathe too deeply
my lungs will collapse
but your hands are steady
like mountain peaks
grounding me
periwinkle posies growing at my feet
and for the first time
I'm breathing air

now my thighs shake
under your sunflower high
    *thunder thighs

Do you fear the thunder as much as I do
the way it feels on your skin
trembling to your bones
with that slow rolling moan
gasping from the heat
are you afraid of the thunder
like you're afraid of me

The way your body moves
is like cascade gold
the way you hold me to the sun
until I come undone
I can't fall fast enough

Don't get too close to the fire
your heart is like rabbit brush on a desert peak
and the fire will leave you
trembling
thirsty without relief
don't get too close to the fire
unless you like the heat

You leave me aching
beating like a heartbeat
the breath of a thousand suns
cascading over my skin
breathing it in and
still find myself gasping for your hands

You leave me breathless and you don't even try
like the way thunder hits your heart
and makes it beat twice
like the wind is dancing with my thighs
safe and wild
at the same time

Take me to pine lined mountainsides
dancing with wildflowers at sunset

I take my new lover to the earth first
to see how they love my mother
do they talk with the trees
do they whisper to leaves and pause
to tell me about the beauty they see
or do they race to the peak
without blinking an eye
do they trample the blooms
and never look at the sky
I take my new lover to the earth first
to see how they love my mother
because I am she
and how you love her
is how you'll love me

watching you drink
from moss-covered waterfalls
the water dripping down your arms
while you laugh
and the sound echoes off the rocks like
the way the sun's rays dance
over the mountain's crown
    *a king

I can see you loved her long before you loved me
*you and the earth

speak to me in the language of lovers
     *wildflowers

Morning sun kissing the soles of my feet
you kissing me
eating flowers from my garden
drinking tea in my chemise
this, my love
is holy
     *communion

I am breathing out daisies
petals falling from my lips
golden tongued
summer love

Tell me about your garden
tell me how you grow so I know
just how to love you

I like to sit in the afterglow
of your sunflower high
your thunderstruck thighs
that make the universe in me shake

I love when the sun goes to sleep
because that is when you start to speak
in whispers that cover my skin
of the things you're afraid to say
in the daylight
    *night

Tell me how the stars live in my skin
how you want to breathe them in

The first time I saw you was a love fight
holding hands down the alley next to midnight
it's too soon to know that I love you but I do
oh my god
I would marry you

I fell in love here
in a single night
in just a few hours I felt like I'd known you
my whole life
and dancing under those golden lights
was alchemy
watching you
watching me
knowing you were afraid to kiss me
knowing you still would

would you dance with me tonight
take me under the blue sky
with strangers walking by
kiss me under the moonlight
I've been fighting this feeling for too long
so dance with me
put your hands on my body
take me to the sea

Moonlit walks
on mountain trails at midnight
down to the water
dipped in starlight
embers dancing in the sky
summer love at midnight

it's you and me now
lighting campfires and
watching the stars fall down
with the taste of red wine
on your lips
watching these hips move slow
tell me you want me
I know you do
lighting campfires
under the moon

there must be something in the moon tonight
all I want is you
dancing in the moonlight
whiskey down
love me right
there must be something in the moon tonight
all I want is you

let's see how long
we can keep the two of us
together under the moon
maybe this time forever

Even in the dark with no moon and no stars
I'd find you
My heart is a compass and you're my true north
At land or the sea as long as your heart is beating
I'd find you

I will always tell you what's on my mind
I don't want to spend my life holding secrets
Keeping them from spilling out the seams in
my skin
I will always say
I love you
Too soon
And fall too fast
And too far
I don't want to spend my life
With wilted whispers on my lips

does your father still sit
in an oversized armchair at 9 pm
next to the fire
with whiskey in his hand
and a cigar in the other
does he tell your new lover
to be careful when she goes to work
how to fight back if it gets out of hand
does he teach her how
to fix the broken sink or
tell her stories from the bayou on Christmas Eve
does he love her like a daughter
the way he loved me?
    *thoughts as I'm fixing my broken sink

you wonder how I remember
so much of the past
small little things like
what you were wearing
painting your room green
and that time you kissed me in the kitchen
the oversized indigo armchair
how loving you was like breathing air
my mind is like a snow globe and
every crystal is a photo
that never melts away
they just fade as they settle to the ground
until someone picks me up and
shakes me around
leaving a constellation of crystals over my head
such small little things these memories

Let's catch feelings like fireflies in July
Hold on for dear life

take me to the coast
to a place only you go
sandy seashell meadows and
spinning in the sea
take me to the coast
to a place only you go

I'm just a creature who loves the sea
salt in my hair and my hair in the wind
waves dancing with my skin
sunkissed oceanside smiles
    *thalassophile

Can we get away just for a few days? I would take even 24 hours if I got to spend it with you. Let's go to a little cabin in the woods and stay up all night, making plans, making love, just being alive. I don't want to miss you. I want to have time with you; make memories and take pictures and tell my friends about you. Be one of those cliches and wear your sweater for days. Wake up and drink coffee and just be. With you. Can we get away just for a few days?

Wild I am
wild I'll be
wild as the mountain
free as the sea
wild I am
wild we'll be
rolling like the river
over me

Let's put up fences between us
maybe that will keep us safe from each other
keep us from getting thirsty
but we end up drinking in the garden
spilling out secrets from our midnight brave
we forgot that fences have gates

you're my blue moon lover
why don't you stay one more night
I don't want to say goodbye
my blue moon lover

you're my blue moon lover
I don't want to say goodbye but
we're running out of time
oh blue moon lover

you're my blue moon lover
kissing daisies in the dark
take me to the stars tonight

you're my blue moon lover
oh you taste like rain in summer and
I'll take you to the stars tonight
blue moon lover

I don't want to wait for the next time
I don't want to pretend like
I'm not falling for you
like stars do

That's the thing about it
I want you every day
In any way I can have you
losing sleep is nothing
to losing time with you and
I will take you
any way I can have you

you feel like sunsets, sunflowers, and sea breeze
and I'd choose you again
you feel like home
safe
with our bodies making waves
salty and sweet
it's no wonder I crave the ocean
when you're made from the sea

waking up with you
is like waking up to summer thunder
your eyes
blinking like butterflies
next to mine
feeling your heart beat steady
your hands moving over my body
making waves
drinking coffee on the porch
while you drink your tea
this is the perfect day
like waking up to summer thunder
two sunflowers
making space for the other to grow
this is how lovers go

We walk a very fine line
between lovers and goodbye
like coral colored wildflowers by the sea
at the end of summer
bittersweet

Let's grow a garden
you and me
we'll plant sunflowers, strawberries, and
peaches by the sea
let's grow a garden
you and me
I don't want you to go this time

summer lovers never last
but damn they sure taste fine
like peaches and tea or cherry wine
and love that takes its time
but they fade away just as soon as they come and
leave your aching bones
oh summer lovers never last

you are my end of summer
sunflower lover
my sun
my sea
my honeybee

You cannot hold the tides
with a lasso for the moon
I won't try
to hold on to you
    *how to say goodbye

these sultry summer
halcyon dreams are just birds
with broken wings

home is where the heart is, they say
they must not have pieces of their heart
scattered all over the place
        *sunflower petals

I will be here
standing in the rain
like I always do
waiting for you
to come back
like sunflowers do

the lovers
sunflowers

Being with you is like dancing with sunflowers
at the end of summer and the stalks leave marks
on your arms
just enough to make them sting
but not bleed
while the petals kiss your cheek until that first
cool breeze blows in
and you wilt

Why are sunflowers
a symbol of joy and adoration
when Clytie stood desperately
on the ground below
waiting for Apollo
to take notice
and the gods pitied her so
seeing her eyes move across the sky and
cry out for love
thirsty for his touch
they couldn't stand to see her beg
enough
they said
if she can't have the sun
perhaps we shall make her one
        *sunflower

careful now
he's a handsome devil and he'll have you
running
in circles with his
smile and
those eyes. those green eyes won me
over and they kept
pulling me in they felt like
home but I should have known it couldn't last
forever and
everything is different now but I'm still
running
in circles

I can't stop imagining my life with you and
maybe none of it would be true and maybe you
could never love me like I think you do

it was summer at the silver lake
where the water is blue like ice
cold like ice
an echo of the sky
how many skulls does the water hold
how many old broken bones
skeletons pulled from closets and
thrown in the water like stones
        *watery grave

I can feel your fingers tugging at the roots
between us
picking at the petals again
you want to grow
just not with me
but you do
or you don't
your indecision is staggering

I have been waiting in the garden
watering the roses
and tender with the weeds
kissing on the wildflowers and
talking to the bees
I have been waiting in the garden
please
my knees are dirty from all the begging
    *stay

loving you is so easy
just like the rain falling
then you evaporate

Easy for you to say
someone
someday
with you
easy for you to say
you're a wildflower
beautiful
free and
you'd make anyone so happy
easy for you to say
when you're the one
walking away

Loving you means letting you go
I should know this by now
you're like the soft breeze at end of summer
where the air is hot and heavy
like the edge of a storm
I should know that loving you
means letting you go

I know what I want
it's you
and if I can't have you
alone
will do

I need you to go but I want you to stay
let's just rip this off like a bandaid
nevermind the scar

you can walk away
but you'll find yourself
right
back
here
with me
I am not so easy to leave

you're always gentle in the way you say goodbye
like you're not sure that this is the last time
will you let the flowers grow or take your pocket
full of posies and run
while I'm left to undo you
like washing off a spider's web

you finally said goodbye after all the times
you said you would but didn't and
I kept thinking that maybe
maybe I was worth it
maybe you would stay and
maybe you would miss my body enough
that you couldn't stay away
but you finally said goodbye after all the times
you said you would
but didn't
and I'm trying to fill this hollow space
with flowers
so I don't numb myself with bodies
because I miss you

I will plant my heart in the garden
where the lovers went to die and
water her with moon soaked rain and
kisses from butterflies
then I'll dance on my own grave
watch these pretty petals bloom
forget-me-nots
forgetting you

oh it's sunset and fireflies tonight
just me and you and the moon and
I don't know how to let you go anymore
or bury these bones
so I'll wake up in the dark
find my way to the stars
they don't fall like you do
I'm used to you leaving
this isn't new to me
we've done this
one
two
three
four times
so can you tell me why you leave
when you keep coming back to me
just to leave

could you really spend the rest of your life
never touching the sea
or climbing the highest peak
is this really
all you want from me

Am I that easy to let go of
watching water slip through your fingers
and the salt doesn't sting you
like it does me
am I that easy to release
tell me
what would make you thirsty

kiss me
like the seas
kiss the shore
dance with me
like the wind does with
the leaves
hold me
like you have no other place to be

I dreamt of you all night
when I was just trying
to get you out of my skin
because it's not the right time
the right place
and I woke up
in the middle of the night realizing
that I could wait my whole life
and it would never be the right time
the right place
and that I was just dreaming
with my eyes awake

I can see the sun coming up
and I want to push him back down
because he wakes you up
and brings you back down to reality
how do you hold both me and responsibility
so delicately
and why is it me
you always release with an apology

one foot
in front of the other
and each step takes me further
in the ice-cold water
I should have known where this would go
we've been here before
while I break my bones and you stand on the
shore and tell me
you can't swim

what is it like to love you
they say
what is it like to touch the sun
what is it like to drink from the sea
     *temporary

and that night
I collided with my past trying to erase the taste
that you left after just fourteen days
when I gave you my heart
to throw into the sea
you left that day with I'm sorry, it's me
I was too much for you
blurring the lines between wrong and so right
that it felt better to you to sever the ties than to
admit this was the best thing between us
how foolish of me
how stupid of you
I cannot believe I let you love me
maybe we were just starving
       *when you left me for California

I almost had you
I could feel you in my fingers
like picking up petals from daisies on the shore
that keep falling
and then she came in
like a summer breeze
love me
love me not
full stop
I could see the wave wash over you
wind wrapped her hold on you
easy
with that breezy summer love
silly me
what was I thinking
I can't compete with a memory
She
a summer breeze and you
the sea
washing away daisies on the shore

no
I'm not ready to let you go
I was never ready
but I've done it before and I'll do it again
because this is what it is to love the sea
and I'll keep wishing it brings you back to me

you think it would be easy
to leave the past behind and
let the petals lie where they fall
death is final
is it not
I didn't know that the memories
were stored in the roots
so instead of getting rid of you
you keep growing back
and wrapping your fingers around my feet

that's the thing about losing someone whose
memory is stored in your skin
you can't just erase it
peel it off and wash it down the drain like you
got a little dirty
as if there's mud on your feet
that's the thing about losing you
you're not just this collection of memories
you're part of me

what am I missing
that I go looking for it in crevices
leaving chasms through my chest
a riptide of goodbyes and regret
what am I missing
that I can't see it through
what am I running from
is it me or is it you

I guess it doesn't make sense to me
you're already there
even though I didn't ask you to be
    *imprint of a ghost

I can still feel you
as I walk by your door
even though you don't live there anymore
and you haven't in years
I can still feel the tears
tearing my heart apart when you said
we'd be better off alone
and though life goes on and
I'm better and stronger
I still miss the way I felt
with you

I hate that you're a ghost in my bed
when you've never even been in it
that I can feel you breathing on my skin
when it's just me laying on these
pale blue sheets

golden leaf canopies
dancing above me
letting in flashes of light
the way they move
sounds like rain or a whisper
and it makes me nervous
I feel like they can hear my bones
aching for yours

I will take you
where the wildflowers go to die
put your lips on mine then
show you the graves
where the honey-tongued liars
took their last breath
    *kiss of death

If you sit still long enough
the birds forget you're there
you just sort of disappear
so I do the same
but about you

how do you move on
when you were never ready to let go
but you went anyway and your memories
left lines in my skin long after the photos were
    ash
and your name still sends
shock waves
echoing through my chest
even though you left not once
not twice
I stopped counting after three
so can you tell me why you left
when you keep coming back to me

I'm still chasing your ghost
I should know better but I don't
I'm still chasing a dream
thinking you could be with me
I'm still in love with your ghost
I should know better but I don't
so I keep chasing a dream
it will be the death of me

I thought I was finally over you
but you came in and took my breath
without trying and I thought I was over you
but I was just empty bones

you
came to me
you
started this conversation
you came to me and I was simply
me
the way I always was with
you and I
sent you running again like I was the one who
poured gasoline at your feet and handed you the
    match
I didn't start the fire and
you
wouldn't be able to handle the heat anyway

you don't spend a second missing me
why should I spend a second missing you
I'm peeling back these layers of a pseudo lover
good under covers
chills down my spine with only whispers and
    sighs
but in the daylight
you're just another kiss goodbye

Why do I keep coming back
to the same place
like visiting my own grave
brace myself for the pain
do I miss the feel of falling
do I like how anger tastes
a dangerous game to play
we both know how this ends

you're standing at my door
end of summer
and I'm watching you
confess your love
too little
too late
I can't stay
my heart can't even break anymore
doesn't even want you anymore
that's when you know the damage is done
when apathy tastes sweeter
than your love

End of summer
comes falling like a waterfall of midnight stars
and I'm crawling out of this
nymphal skeleton
Leaving you
Like cicada do

watching the sun set over the sea thinking
maybe it was me
maybe it was me
watching the waves crash over my feet
washing you clean

what is it like to die
I've already lost you
a hundred times
planting sunflowers every time you leave
thinking maybe this time
the bloom will take
maybe this time
you'll last the summer
and the wind won't break your spine
but I'd be lyin'
so I'll keep
planting sunflowers til I die

loving her
bones

let it out
give the thunder something to shake about

I used to reject the idea that people could break.
I was too strong, too aware, and too alive to be so
brittle. But fractures started forming in my skin
and all it would take is one last push, one last
fall, to see that I, the unbroken, was breaking.

the sky like velvet on my skin
soft and heavy
pulling me in
but pulling me under
the moon reaching for light
coming for mine
but I'm tired of being the sun
can I be the rain for a while now

let the tears come spilling out over the edge
a waterfall of salt and regret
let the tears come like a river
so they don't make caverns in your chest

what you should do
what you should want
where you should stay
    *a cage

It's late and
I can't sleep
my feet are freezing like I'm ready to take flight
instead of staying to fight These Demons
dancing on the edge of my head
and the adrenaline makes me nauseous
like a caution sign that I fully ignore telling me to
stay away and instead I
open the gate

walking down a path lined with trees
beasts and monsters following me
kicking up dust at my feet and
whispering in my ear
this way, my dear
as they lead me to the cliffs

butterflies like the taste of decay
maybe this is why I'm drawn to half dead men
who pick out my heart to fill their rotting bones
then ask me what's next
but I am not your home

what is it like to love everyone but yourself
like walking around with a bouquet of summer
     flowers
and watching the blooms disappear one by one
     and in the end
you're left with empty stems

why do I go looking for your light
in my mirror when my eyes start getting dimmer
    *validation

always on the run
looking for love
in all the wrong places
such a cliche
how did you ever get
away from yourself

it's easier to love you
than it is to love me
why is that
is it because I have been conditioned to think
that your needs are above my own
that your thirst be met first
at the expense of my body
as many times as you'd like and that
it doesn't matter what I want
as long as
you
are satisfied

do you like your body
yes I replied
but you asked me so many times
that I wondered if you didn't believe me
as if it was you that needed convincing

things look better they say
and they are
because I was willing to put down my gun
and say
okay
you win this fight
offer myself up to chains
just so things would stay the same

raindrops
dripping on my head
as I sit at your grave trying to listen to what
    you'd said
and so sad you couldn't stay
what would you say to this
you
who'd had two loves
both who could never love you like you deserved
yet you stayed
tell me why
and if I should do the same

I led you to the water
stepping softly over the worn down path
through sun-soaked trees down to the water
the flowers have grown tired
so I blow them a kiss and whisper
don't drop your petals just yet
as I led you to the water then watched you
stepping to the edge
trampling over the flowers
kicking rocks in
while I'm looking up at sun-soaked trees
I led you to the water
and you still refused to drink

I used to think that love was good enough
that loving you would show you
how to love me back
but all it did was show you
I was delicate and
every Sunflower Fades
if you let it

Do you want to know what it's like to die
while you're alive?
like choking on air
when you're just trying to breathe

he's eating up my flesh and gnawing at my bones
    *time

you and me
it's a desert
and one of us is thirsty for the sea

I don't know how to say goodbye
when we never really came home
I don't know how to make myself love you
when I don't
and I don't know why
you'd want to stay caged
when you said you have wings

I've got salt on my lips from the blood coming up
from the break in my heart that you tried to stop
with watered-down apologies and flowers
that will die soon anyway
you know I loathe roses
empty promises again
I should know by now
it's nothing new
the same old you

do you know how to find me when it gets dark
and I can't send out the stars anymore
because I'm falling into the sea with my eyes
    closed
and the cold puts me to sleep
do you know how to find me and
bring me back from the deep

you can't lie to the body that holds your soul
it knows when you're dying
even if you don't

I feel like I'm constantly swimming to the surface of the sea and saying, there she is, there's me, only to watch her gasp for air, another deep inhale before the next wave takes her down. How long does it take a soul to drown?

I'll take the fall
I'm used to falling anyway
out of love
out of time
out of grace
so I'll take the fall

Here comes the witch of the wood
they say she danced with the devil
and now she's got blood on her hands
so light your fires up
go get 'em, love
bring back her heart
then tie her up and burn the witch of the wood

Here comes the witch of the wood
they say she danced with the devil
and I should have known it was true
the way she looked at you
licking her lips
watching you fall into her kiss
here comes the witch of the wood

here comes the witch of the wood
oh I danced with the devil
and I own this blood on my hands
so light your fires up
come get me, love
bring back my heart
then tie me up and burn the witch of the wood

they say she carries their bones and
made love to the moon
you better run or she'll catch you too
and turn you into stone

I've been walking through the valleys and
the bone trodden alleys trying to get your blood
up off me but it's marked me for the wolves

I used to watch the women cry
and wonder how they looked so pretty
because my tears let the demons loose
and maybe they don't have any
but I do
and they come tearing out my eyes
plunging to their death
until the River runs dry
I used to watch the women cry
and wonder how they looked so pretty
because my tears let the demons loose
and maybe they don't have any
but I do

I know my sins
and I know
that you think I
should suffer more
Hellfire
Brimstone
How dare you
How could you
           Cast your stones
Say you're sorry
           I'm sorry
             Guilty
Say it again
I want to see you bleed
maybe this will make you love me
    *confession

tell me it's over
tell me it's done
tell me it's my fault
my fault
my fault
you've already won
you think this is easy
it's like digging my own grave
while I'm buried awake

what do you see when you look at me
is it only skin and sin
what do you see
can you get past your
holy apologies
gasping for air through your prayers
what do you see
when you look at me
    *demons

the fire turned to ashes
ashes turned to dust
and it's such a shame that
it wasn't enough

When will you stop
breathing down my neck
the Devil's dripping tongue
desperate

maybe you should say nothing at all
is your preaching
more important than my peace
is turning me to dust
more important than your love
maybe you should say nothing at all
because the louder you are
the harder you'll fall

You couldn't kill me if you tried
I've been dancing with devils my whole life

sometimes I look at my face
and I see you in my cheeks
and in my hair
in the copper of my skin and
in the shape of my chin
and when my eyes get dark
I see you the most then
I hear you in my ears when
I'm looking in the glass
watching shadows dance on my shoulders
it's no wonder you couldn't stand the sight of me
when I was the mirror for your
antipathy

I know you want to forget that I exist
but my body, my breath
gave life to the flowers
you hold in your hands
so you can't

how was I supposed to know
that slamming doors was saying goodbye
you did it all the time
and he still let you home
how was I to know
that your love
was not a map to follow

I have spent a lifetime undoing the spells
you spoke over me with your serpent tongue
this is why I picked up snakes
rattles and all
I wasn't afraid of the bite
I've been cleaning them out my whole life

this energy is not mine to carry
these bones are not mine to bury
and you can kick and scream
how could you do this to me
but I was standing on the side
and this was never about me
it was always about you

I am tired of planting flowers over the holes
you keep digging
just to find more in the garden
the same hole in a different place
aren't you tired of your diatribe
doesn't your body ache from all the digging
aren't your fingers broken enough
how are you still thirsty for blood

aren't you tired
of telling the same lies
the same story all the time
aren't you tired
of blowing smoke
choking on the grapes
that you've picked from the vine
aren't you tired

the earth is groaning
under the weight of your whispers

when did the wild stop feeling safe
when did we
start putting ourselves in cages
by choice
when did we stop daring to go outside
when did we decide that we wanted
to be tamed
and only a few names held the keys
what happened to you
what happened to me
I am taking my wild back
I do not care if you scream

I don't need protection anymore
I made sure of that
never again would I trust someone so close to me
or so close to you
keep your friends close
your enemies closer they say
but I won't be within arms reach when you try
and bury me

I was waiting for daisies
hoping you'd bring them home
when I could have grown them myself
I won't be waiting for love anymore

I do not need your hands to touch me
I have my own
and they love me better than you ever did

I didn't know I could see stars in the daylight
or that I was dripping honey
    *golden touch

I can feel my fingers breaking open
as the rock cuts through and the dirt seeps in
while the river below waits to water my bones
but I'm hanging on by the roots.

Help
there's been a murder
what an unkindness in the middle of day
a tiding of what's to come
a trembling
send in the squadrons they chime with a wisdom
a murmuration between the trees
a glittering in the sky as they cry
help
there's been a murder

Here I am on the forest floor
covered in leaves and decay
but this is how
life is made

Can you feel your roots
trembling in the meadow
the quaking leaves whispering
don't be afraid
it is safe here
stay
      *awake

the ground stops shaking and
my pulse is still beating
I'm looking up at lost trees
wandering feet that brought me here
I've found myself

I came to a fork in the road
and both signs screamed
come this way
it will be better one day
you'll see
stay
but I looked away and up at the sky and said
I'd rather fly
so I gave myself wings

loving her started from the death of her old loves
the ones that swallowed her up and trapped her
at midnight
loving her
came from goodbye

loving her
marigolds

Through cliffs and stones and buried bones
I am growing into marigolds

My spine is made of stems
growing flowers from my ribs
wrapping around my neck and
holding my head high
wearing this crown of butterflies

will you stay soft
when they pick your petals
maybe some days
but not always
and not today

I am leaving butterfly kisses
on flowers that I grew from my body
and you have the audacity to try
and pick them for yourself
to spit on the soil they were planted in
the rain they are fed
whispering do you see what she did
did you hear what she said
kicking up dirt
to cover up the sun
I may let the first cut ache before taking aim
but I am not your prey
and I will not run
from wolves like you

go on my love
pick up your crown off the ground
do you see how it shines through the dirt
how even the mud can't cover it up
    *April showers bring May flowers

you brought the rain
so I planted seeds
you called in the thunder
so I took out the weeds
you shook the ground
and I stood mine
no more
not this time
        *aries

I am the type of woman who is willing to say,
enough. even when my voice cracks and my body
shakes. that is not fear you hear; it's my brave.

I will not settle
like stones in the river or
bury my bones in the forest floor
I will not be waiting at your door
peddling for pennies to make wishes
in the puddles you left in place of your love

I will not sacrifice myself to you anymore
holding my breath until I'm blue
suffocating for you
like you're some god
when I am all love on my own
I will not lay down or fall to my knees
Like you expect me to
I am not sacrificing myself to you

I carry the strength of warriors in my bones and
I feel their chants run through my blood and the
sweat drip down my arms while my body shakes
like an echo of ocean waves dancing through a
cave. I am the light that shines off the moon.
I am the wildflower on the mountain that still
blooms and I carry the strength of warriors in my
bones.

I was born a flower child
quiet and wild
in love with the sun
and salty air
and whispering pines
the rain isn't going to hurt me this time

I used to breathe my I love yous into colored
glass bottles and put them on the shelf so they
didn't come spilling out and make rainbows over
your rain clouds. But you can't stop the sun from
shining and now these colored glass bottles are
free. Spilling out I love yous and making
rainbows out of rain clouds

she comes between
sunset and midnight in the summer
calling to the moon
such a delicate love
an ephemeral fall into the desert
      *bloom

my roots are coming up silver
you didn't know I was made of stars

do you ever wonder about the moon
what would it be like
if you cut her in two
just to see what's inside
and act surprised when you find
that she was full of stars
    *why do you do this to yourself

I'm afraid of getting lost
so I leave bits of cosmic dust
on everything I touch and
they light up like a trail of stars
when it starts to get too dark
        *starlight

as I've been writing I've been wondering
why is it easier to love them than it is to love me
how can I write so quickly
so easily
about someone who is not even mine
am I so detached from my own peace
my own divine body
that I cannot see it for what it is
see me for what I give
why is it easier to love them
than it is to love me
    *conditioning

it's easier to cover the mirror
with photos of past lovers and say
see all the ones I've loved before
of course I love myself
but loving the lovers is not enough
you must learn to love yourself
     *true love

How does love grow
a little at a time
with grit and some spine
bloody hands from fist fights in the mirror
and the beasts in my mind
how does love grow
     *it's a fight

ever since I was young it was like
my body didn't belong to me
don't dress like that or talk that way
you'll draw attention to yourself
I am eleven
what do you mean
what is there to see
I am not responsible for the actions
of ravenous fools
whistling at a child from their pick up trucks
I am eleven
covered in sweats that are too big for my body
what is there to see
what do you mean
does this body even belong to me or
was it only made for the eyes of hungry ghosts
gobbling up my flesh
making it their home when they
were never invited in
I am eleven
what is there to see
ever since I was young it was like my body didn't
belong to me
first him
then them
and only now is it becoming home again

When we met I was carrying skeletons
growing flowers between my ribs and
you gave me sunshine and kissed me with
warm summer rain
being with you showed me
all of the love I had
growing from the seams
then we faded like flowers do
seeds blowing into secret gardens
growing new roots
and the flowers between my ribs
could never find the sun
no matter how many times I planted seeds and
kissed them with warm summer rain
I was carrying skeletons I couldn't keep away
and I found myself sleeping in
empty graves saying take me away
one last time
I closed my eyes
then saw the sun was within and started growing
marigolds from new stems
so when you came back like a chelidonian wind
and whispered oh
you look just like I imagined
I knew I was home again
growing flowers from these skeletons
     *new skin

Now I dance
naked in the mirror
like sunflowers
in the summer

unbecoming who I thought
I was supposed to be
how I thought I was supposed to feel
and what I was supposed to do
removing the cage
breaking chains
taking chances on making mistakes
letting myself fall into empty space
I'm used to falling anyway and
I'm not afraid of skinned knees

I'm shedding my skin again
and you call me a snake
but this is what snakes do
shedding skin
is just me growing again
     *rebirth

you never know what fires
you are lighting behind you
as you go up in flames and turn to ash
embers that leave them trembling in your wake
asking questions that they never dared to say
before you caught fire and showed them you
were okay in the end
    *phoenix

You will find that there is peace in the fire

loving her didn't come easy
she had to fight off the wolves
that were hungry for a casualty

Learn to fall in love with yourself
over and over again
you are the one who will always be there
through every tragedy and heartbreak
so learn to fall in love with yourself
over and over again
pick yourself up and clean your scraped knees
find what makes you happy even when you're
alone learn to fall in love with yourself
over and over again
you are your home

It has been far too long since I have seen the sea
and felt the salt on my skin
sticky sweet
rising tides in the moonlight calling me home
come dip your toes in these waves they say
it has been far too long
since we have held you

The sun kisses my lips
hands dancing with the sky
and this is the year I find myself whole
even here
alone

Stay high on this love
on this feeling of being enough
stay high on this touch of magic
glittering on your skin
stay high on the good shit

Everyone carries pain in their pocket
but happiness
happiness is like catching fireflies
delicate dreams of light dancing in the dark
keeping them in jars
and once we have it
we question it
how long will this last
this can't be real
so we watch it
even will it to fade away
bury them deep
because pain is easier to keep
but tonight I will watch that light
dancing in the dark and
let it cover me like liquid gold
    *breaking cycles

Today I will be gentle to her like I'm growing a
garden from my hips and I'll speak love spells
over her as if I'm watering her with my lips
      *to myself

The way my body moves is like cascade gold
    *loving you showed me how to love myself

dark hair
dark lips
sweeter than molasses kiss
thick thighs and honey hips
brown eyes
brown skin
god, I love the body I'm in

I want to be in a cottage by the sea
just exist without the expectation
of doing more
or doing less
than breathing
I just want to exist
sit here in this dress and dream
eat fish from the sea
lie down in this body
and let the sun cover me
dance under the stars
until the embers breathe out
living in a cottage by the sea

Breezy summer day
falling asleep in the sun
all I ever need

Now I am taller than the trees
With roots made of daydreams
and butterfly wings
Now I am breathing in the sun and the sea
Singing with the birds
Haven't you heard
    *she's free

I was made for the mountains
the mountains were made for me
you see, we were made for each other
the mountain peaks and me

I am made of butterflies, bones, and smoke
salty and sweet
conquering peaks and
picking wildflowers in bare feet
easy summer sunsets and meeting strangers in
strange places and drinking up moonlight
dancing wild with the sea
watching stars fall from the sky while laying on
the concrete still holding that afternoon heat
salty and sweet
butterflies, bones, and smoke

Sun shines through dragonfly wings
their feet kiss the tickseed
dancing in the marmalade breeze
    *peace

Stardust and pink sunsets
tangerine skies
salty air kissing my thighs
flowing like the sea
strong like the mountains behind me
breathe
        *when I finally exhale

It's been
three thousand three hundred sixty three days
since I've felt awake
like a cool summer morning
on the brink of change
where the air is soft enough to brush against your
skin and feel like a kiss
the kind where your lips almost touch but miss
I've been dying for so long I forgot what it's like
to feel alive
is this what breathing feels like

Maybe healing is like climbing a mountain.
A lot of starting and stopping and getting lost.
You fall down, get bruised, maybe try a new path.
Some days you feel strong. Other days, not
enough. Then you find yourself at the top. God,
the view up here. The air up here. Your lungs
are expanding and your thighs are shaking, but
goddamn, you made it and today you are
stronger. You sit here for a while. Smell the
flowers, rest, recharge. Then you see the storm
rolling in. Quick. Take cover. You start your way
down. Thrashing through brambles, getting cut
on the thorns, just trying to stay ahead of the
storm. Maybe healing is like climbing a mountain
and maybe the next time it will be easier to find
your way.

I stopped picking at the flowers
growing from my scars
and let the weeds go free
now my body is a garden
I belong to me

thank you, xo
Alisha

IG : @whereshegrows

Also by the author:

Still Growing Wildflowers

www.ingramcontent.com/pod-product-compliance
Lightning Source LLC
Chambersburg PA
CBHW071311140726
47996CB00005B/1726